W9-ATP-679

Down on the Farm

DUCKS

Sally Morgan

QEB Publishing

First published in the United States by
QEB Publishing, Inc.
23062 La Cadena Drive
Laguna Hills, CA 92653

www.qeb-publishing.com

Library of Congress Control Number: 2007001488

ISBN 978 1 59566 387 0

Written by Sally Morgan
Designed by Tara Frese
Editor Corrine Ochiltree
Picture Researcher Nic Dean
Illustrations by Chris Davidson

Publisher Steve Evans
Creative Director Zeta Davies
Senior Editor Hannah Ray

Printed and bound in China

Picture credits

Key: t = top, b = bottom, c = center,
l = left, r = right, FC = front cover, BC = back cover

Alamy /Renee Morris 5, /Arco Images 8, 9, 22, /Oote
Boe Photography 11, /Papilio 12 tl, /Chris George 16 tl,
/Beaconstox 19; **Ardea** /John Daniels title page, 10,
/Andy Teare 6; **Corbis** /Randy M. Ury FC, /A. Inden
15 ct, /Keren Su 16 br, /18 bl Reuters; **Ecoscene** Sally
Morgan 17 tr; **FLPA** /Flip De Nooyer/Foto Natural
5 bl, /Frank W. Lane 17 bl; **Getty Images** G. K.
Hart/Vikki Hart/The Image Bank BC, /altrendo
nature 4, /Dave King/Dorling Kindersley 12 br, /Luzia
Ellert/StockFood Creative 13, /Guy Edwardes/The
Image Bank 14, /www.korean-arts.com 18 tr;
Photolibrary Group Ltd 7

CONTENTS

Words in **bold** can be found in the Glossary on page 22.

Ducks on the farm

Do you know where the soft feathers in a snuggly feather pillow and **comforter** come from? Many of these feathers come from ducks.

A mother duck swimming with her ducklings.

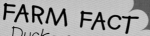

A group of Aylesbury ducks.

FARM FACT
Ducks can see almost all the way around them without having to turn their heads.

Ducks are found on farms all around the world. They are very useful birds. They give us meat, eggs, and feathers. Ducks can help farmers, too. They gobble up a lot of slugs and snails that like to eat farmers' crops.

Ducks from beak to tail

The largest ducks can grow up to 16 in. (40 cm) long, from shoulder to tail, and can weigh as much as 13 lbs. (6 kg). That's the same weight as six bags of sugar.

Eye

Body covered in feathers

Wings for flying

Beak

Tail

Webbed feet for swimming

This drake has curly tail feathers.

Height of six-year-old child

Height of duck

Male ducks are called **drakes**, female ducks are called ducks, and baby ducks are called **ducklings**.

Some drakes are more colorful than ducks and have curly feathers on their tails.

7

It's a duck's life...

A duck starts life inside an egg. The female duck lays eggs in a nest. Then, she sits on them to keep them warm.

The ducklings **hatch** after 28 days. Each duckling makes a hole in its shell with a special egg tooth at the end of its beak. It cracks open the shell and pushes itself out. A duckling can run around within minutes of hatching.

These newly hatched ducklings have fluffy feathers.

FARM FACT
Some ducks live for a long time. One white drake living in Wales reached the amazing age of 25!

Ducklings replace their fluffy feathers with stiff, adult feathers when they grow up.

A baby duck has all its grown-up feathers by the time it is about seven weeks old.

A female duck starts to lay eggs during her first spring. Ducks can live for two to fifteen years, depending on how many eggs they lay.

Dabbling ducks

Ducks like to play in mud and make a mess! They push their beaks into the mud to look for small animals to eat, such as worms and snails.

Ducks also love swimming. They have large, **webbed** feet that are perfect for paddling around in water.

Ducks cannot feel the cold through their feet.

Sometimes a duck bobs up and down on the water with its head under the surface and its tail in the air. This is called **dabbling**.

A duck dabbles so that its head can reach the bottom of the pond to look for food.

Eggs and meat

Female ducks lay large, white eggs. They are about twice the size of chicken eggs. Most ducks lay their eggs during spring and summer, although some lay eggs all year round.

A good, egg-laying duck may lay more than 300 eggs in a year! Duck eggs can be eaten, just like chicken eggs.

Duck eggs can be used to make yummy cakes.

Duck is popular in Chinese cooking.

Some types of ducks grow very large, such as the Aylesbury and Peking ducks. These ducks are kept in special farms and used for meat. There are lots of these farms in Southeast Asia and China. These ducks grow quickly and can get very fat!

Wonderfully warm

A mallard drake in flight.

A duck has different types of feathers. It has a layer of smooth feathers that covers its body. The long feathers on its wings are called flight feathers. They help a duck fly. Small, fluffy feathers called down feathers lie next to a duck's skin.

An eiderdown is a type of comforter filled with down feathers. It is named after the Eider duck.

FARM FACT
A mallard duck can take off almost **vertically** (upward) from water. This means that it can fly over any trees growing beside the water without hitting them.

The Eider is a wild duck that lives in places where temperatures fall below freezing. It has very, very warm feathers!

15

Different ducks

INDIAN RUNNER

This is a tall duck that stands very upright. It is nicknamed "penguin duck" because it stands a little like a penguin.

MAYA

The Maya duck comes from China. Flocks of Maya ducks are herded onto fields of rice. The ducks feed on insects and other small animals living around the rice to help protect the crops from harm.

MAGPIE DUCK

This duck has
white feathers with
blue-gray patches
on its head and body.
It lays blue eggs.

CRESTED DUCK

The **crested** duck has
a puff of feathers that
sticks up on its head.
Some look like they
are wearing little hats!
Crested ducks come
in different colors.

17

Duck customs

KOREA

It is a **tradition** in Korea to give a pair of **carved** ducks as a wedding present for good luck. If the married couple is happy, they place the ducks so they face each other. If they are unhappy, the ducks look away from each other.

SINGAPORE

Many people around the world hold duck races. In Singapore, plastic ducks are let go on a river and float **downstream**. The owner of the duck that crosses the finish line first wins a prize.

18

CHINA

Each autumn, Chinese people celebrate the Moon Festival. It is traditional to eat Moon Cakes during the festival. There are different types of Moon Cakes, but one type has a cooked duck egg yolk inside. People eat the cakes at night, under a full moon.

Quacking good fun

Make your own cute duck. You will need a paper plate, a sheet of yellow paper, a sheet of orange cardstock, pencil, paints, paintbrushes, scissors, glue, feathers (optional), and a black pen.

1 Paint one side of the paper plate yellow and fold it in half. The yellow color should be on the outside. Press firmly along the fold.

2 Place the sheet of yellow paper on a table and trace your hand twice with a pencil.

3 Ask a grown-up to cut out the two hand shapes. These shapes form the tail feathers. Glue them into position on each side of the plate.

4 Draw a beak and legs with webbed feet on the orange cardstock. Ask a grown-up to cut them out for you. Glue the beak and the legs to the plate.

5 Paint wings on both sides of the plate. Glue feathers onto the wings. Draw on two eyes with a black pen.

21

Glossary and Index

carved shaped by cutting with a knife or sharp blade

comforter a large bedcover, often filled with feathers

crest feathers that stick up on the head of a duck

dabbling when ducks push their beaks into mud underwater to look for food

downstream the direction in which the water in a river or stream flows

drake a male duck

duckling a baby duck

gland part of a duck's body that makes special oil, which the duck uses to make its feathers waterproof

hatch when a duckling breaks out of its egg

preening when a duck cleans its feathers with its beak

tradition a custom or way of doing something that is passed from parent to child

vertically straight up or down

webbed joined by pieces of skin that make it easy to swim

23

Ideas for teachers and parents

- Read about the different breeds of ducks. Make fact sheets about the children's favorite breeds. Find out which ones are used for meat and which ones are kept for eggs.

- Visit a waterfowl or poultry center where children can see different breeds of ducks. A good time to visit is late spring or early summer, when there will be ducklings as well as adult ducks. Some centers allow children to go into the incubator rooms to see ducklings hatch.

- Visit local ponds with the children to see wild ducks.

- Look inside a pillow containing feathers. Take one of the feathers and look at how it is constructed. Puff up the down pillow or comforter to show how comforters and pillows trap air and help keep you warm.

- Make a collage of a duck. Take a large piece of white paper and draw the outline of a duck on it. Look through old magazines and cut out any pictures of ducks, ducklings, and feathers. Collect scraps of material and natural or artificial feathers. Stick these inside the outline to make a colorful duck.

- Make a word search using the duck-related vocabulary in this book.

- Compare duck eggs with chicken eggs. Duck eggs can be bought in some supermarkets or from farm stores. Weigh a duck egg. See how easy it is to break the egg open. Compare the weight and ease of breaking with a chicken egg. Make two batches of scrambled eggs, one with duck eggs and one with chicken eggs. Ask the children if they can taste any difference.

- Ask the children to think of the names of famous ducks that appear in books, poems, and cartoons, for example Donald Duck. Encourage them to write a poem about a duck.

PLEASE NOTE

Check that each child does not have an egg intolerance before carrying out the scrambled egg activity above.

24